THE WORLD'S GREATEST
MOTORBIKES

Ian Graham

Raintree

www.raintreepublishers.co.uk
Visit our website to find out more information about Raintree books.

To order:
☎ Phone 44 (0) 1865 888112
📄 Send a fax to 44 (0) 1865 314091
💻 Visit the Raintree Bookshop at www.raintreepublishers.co.uk to browse our
catalogue and order online.

First published in Great Britain by Raintree,
Halley Court, Jordan Hill, Oxford, OX2 8EJ, part
of Harcourt Education.
Raintree is a registered trademark of Harcourt
Education Ltd.

Editorial: Andrew Farrow and Dan Nunn
Design: Ron Kamen and Philippa Baile
Picture Research: Hannah Taylor and Elaine
  Willis
Production: Duncan Gilbert

Originated by Dot Gradations Ltd.
Printed in China

The paper used to print this book comes from
sustainable resources.

13 dig ISBN 978 1844 21 262 0
10 dig ISBN 1 844 21262 9
10 09 08 07 06
10 9 8 7 6 5 4 3 2

**British Library Cataloguing in Publication
Data**
Graham, Ian, 1953-
  Motorbikes. – (The world's greatest)
  1. Motorcycles – Juvenile literature
  I. Title
  629.2'275
A full catalogue record for this book is
available from the British Library.

Acknowledgements
The publishers would like to thank the
following for permission to reproduce
photographs:

American Suzuki Motor Corporation pp. **6**, **7
top**, **7 bottom**, **8 bottom**; Associated Press
pp. **21**, **24 bottom**; Cagivausa p. **19**; Corbis
pp. **5** (Bettmann), **14** (Reuters/Michael
Kooren), **24 top** (Bettmann); Daimler Chrysler
p. **25**; Dave Campos p. **22**; Ducati pp. **10**, **11**;
Getty Images pp. **4** (AFP/Jim Watson), **16**
(Allsport/Mike Cooper), **17** (Allsport/Mike
Cooper), **18** (AFP/Dimitar Dilkoff), **20**
(Jonathan Ferry); Honda pp. **8 top**, **9**;
Landracing.com p. **23**; Ronald Grant Archive
p. **13 bottom**; The Car Photo Library pp. **12**
(David Kimber), **13 top** (David Kimber);
Yamaha pp. **1**, **15**.

Cover photograph of Valentino Rossi on his
Honda Moto GP bike, October 2003, reproduced
with permission of Corbis/Reuters/Heino Kalis.

Every effort has been made to contact
copyright holders of any material reproduced
in this book. Any omissions will be rectified in
subsequent printings if notice is given to the
publishers.

Contents

Words appearing in the text in bold, **like this**, are explained in the Glossary.

Motorbikes

There are many kinds of motorbikes. Millions of people all over the world ride them.

Types of motorbikes

Some motorbikes are for riding on roads. Motorbikes called **cruisers** and **tourers** are comfortable for long journeys. **Sports bikes** are more fun and exciting to ride, but they are not as comfortable. Other bikes are for riding off the road and for racing. Motocross bikes are tall, light bikes for bumpy, muddy ground. Racing bikes are built to go very fast on a special race-track.

Motorcycles today have two wheels and an engine in the middle, just like the Daimler Einspur (see right). But modern bikes are stronger and more powerful. They are also easier to ride and have better brakes.

When did it all begin?

The first motorcycle was built in Germany by Gottlieb Daimler in 1885. Daimler made a wooden bicycle and added a small petrol engine. The bike was called the Einspur.

Motorcycles have changed a lot since the Einspur. Compare Daimler's motorbike with a modern one like the Honda Fireblade!

Daimler's Einspur motorcycle was ridden for the first time by his son Paul on 10 November 1885.

	Daimler Einspur	Honda CBR1000RR Fireblade
Built in:	1885	2005
Engine:	265 cc/16 cu in	998 cc/61 cu in
Power:	0.5 horsepower	170 horsepower
Top speed:	12 kph/8 mph	286 kph/178 mph

The fastest road bike

The world's fastest road bike is the Suzuki GSX1300R Hayabusa. It has a powerful engine. But a powerful engine isn't enough to make a motorbike go really fast. The reason the Hayabusa can go so fast is because it has a really smooth shape.

Beating drag

When a motorbike moves, it goes through the air. The air pushes back and slows it down. The push of the air against the bike is called **drag**. Some shapes make a lot of drag. The smooth shape of the Hayabusa means the drag is very small. This makes it go very fast.

The Hayabusa and its rider have a very smooth shape.

SPEEDY FLIER

The Suzuki Hayabusa is named after a bird. The body of the Hayabusa falcon has a perfect shape so that it can dive through the air at over 300 kph (186 mph). That's the same speed as the bike!

Suzuki GSX1300R Hayabusa

Engine: 1,299 cc/79 cu in
Power: 173 horsepower
Weight: 217 kg/478 lb
Top speed: 312 kph/194 mph

The wedge-shaped nose slices easily through the air at high speed.

A motorbike engine needs air to burn its fuel. Holes on each side of the Hayabusa's nose let lots of air flow to the engine.

Other fast road bikes

There are many fast motorcycles for the road. They are called sports road bikes. The fastest include the Honda Fireblade, the Honda Super Blackbird, and the Suzuki GSX-R1000.

Black beauty

The Honda Super Blackbird was once the fastest road motorcycle. Its engine is as big as some car engines. The Super Blackbird is bigger and heavier than other sports road bikes. It is also more comfortable to ride.

The Super Blackbird is still one of the world's fastest motorbikes.

The Suzuki GSX-R1000 is very light for its size, so it is very fast too.

Fast Fireblade

The Honda Fireblade is one of the most popular sports road bikes today. It is lighter than other road bikes the same size. This helps to make it faster. It also makes it more exciting to ride. The Fireblade has been changed over the years to keep it up to date. Today it has a bigger and more powerful engine.

The latest Honda Fireblade has a bigger engine than the first Fireblade and it goes faster.

	Honda Super Blackbird	Honda Fireblade
Engine:	1,137 cc/69 cu in	998 cc/61 cu in
Power:	150 horsepower	170 horsepower
Weight:	227 kg/500 lb	179 kg/395 lb
Top speed:	300 kph/186 mph	286 kph/178 mph

The most desirable road bike

The Ducati 999R is a road motorbike that lots of people would like to ride. They would like to ride the racing version too!

Superbike!

Ducati bikes are famous for being beautiful and fast. They have been very successful in **Superbike** racing. The Ducati bike used in Superbike racing today is the Ducati 999. It is the racing version of the Ducati 999R road bike. To make the racing bike, nearly every part of the road bike was slimmed down or made from a different material to make it lighter.

The Ducati 999's streamlined shape was designed by computers. The bike in this photo is the Superbike racing version.

NEAT NOSE

One of the lights at the front of the Ducati 999R is above the other. This makes the bike's nose narrower, so it cuts through the air better at high speeds.

A Ducati 999 road bike leans over to take a turn at high speed.

	Ducati 999R	**Ducati 999F05**
Type of bike:	**Road bike**	Superbike racer
Engine:	**999 cc/61 cu in**	999 cc/61 cu in
Power:	**150 horsepower**	194 horsepower
Weight:	**192 kg/423 lb**	165 kg/364 lb
Top speed:	**275 kph/170 mph**	300 kph/186 mph

The coolest motorbike

There are fashions in motorbikes just like fashions in clothes and music. Some motorbikes are "cooler" than others. Many people think the coolest motorbikes are Harley-Davidsons. They are often just called Harleys or hogs.

Classic styling

Harley-Davidson has been making motorbikes for more than 100 years. Unlike other motorbike makers, it has kept the same style. Today, the classic Harley-Davidson style is cooler and more popular than ever. One of the best-selling Harleys is the Road King. It is a very comfortable bike for riding long distances.

Harley-Davidson Road King

Engine: 1,449 cc/88 cu in
Weight: 332 kg/732 lb
Length: 2.4 m/8 ft
Wheelbase: 1.6 m/5 ft 3 in

The Road King is a very comfortable bike for riding long distances. Cruisers like the Road King are longer and heavier than sports bikes.

Potato engine

Harleys have an engine called a **V-twin**. It is called this because the **fuel** is burned in two **cylinders** joined at the bottom to make a V shape. If you want to know what a big V-twin Harley engine sounds like, just say "potato-potato-potato-potato"!

The Harley-Davidson Electra Glide is one of the best-equipped touring bikes there is. It has its own stereo music system. It also has an intercom to let the rider and passenger talk to each other.

Harley owners often make their bikes look different from everyone else's. This is called customising. The most famous type of customised Harley was the 1970s "chopper". The chopper had long handlebars called "ape-hangers"!

The fastest racing bikes

The fastest and most exciting motorcycle races are **MotoGP** races. Bikes are made especially for MotoGP racing. The races take place all over the world.

Turning on the power

MotoGP rules say the bikes can have 990 cc (60 cu in) engines. These engines are very powerful. A MotoGP bike like the Yamaha YZR-M1 can reach over 325 kph (202 mph).

MotoGP riders lean their bikes over to steer them around a turn. The tyres have to grip the track even at these crazy angles.

Yamaha YZR-M1 MotoGP racing bike

Engine:	**990 cc/60 cu in**
Power:	**240 horsepower**
Top speed:	**over 325 kph/202 mph**

Staying on track

A rider has to use his engine's power carefully. A bike will spin and tumble off the track if the rider goes too fast around a turn or **accelerates** too quickly.

windshield

fairing

*The Yamaha YZR-M1 is one of the best MotoGP racing bikes. In this photo, the rider is tucked in behind the **fairing** and windshield. This helps air to flow smoothly over the bike and rider.*

15

Sidecar racers

Some road bikes carry an extra passenger in a **sidecar**.
The sidecar looks like a seat with a wheel. People
often race motorbikes and sidecars. Road bikes and
sidecars are made separately and then joined. A racing
bike and sidecar are made together as one vehicle.
The motorbike and front of the sidecar have a
streamlined body called a fairing.

The rider and passenger
crouch down behind
the motorcycle and
sidecar body as they
speed along a straight
part of the track.

Staying upright

A motorbike leans over to help it turn. But a motorbike with a sidecar can't lean over. It has to stay upright. The passenger in a racing sidecar leans over as far as possible towards the inside of each turn. This stops the bike from toppling over. It also lets the bike take turns faster.

Flat-top tyres

Racing sidecars have tyres that are very wide and flat. This produces the most grip so that they can go round turns faster.

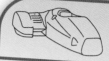

Sidecar racer

Length:	2.7 m/8 ft 10 in
Height:	75 cm/2 ft 6 in
Weight:	375 kg/825 lb
Engine:	1,000 cc/61 cu in
Power:	180 horsepower
Top speed:	280 kph/175 mph

As the motorcycle turns, the passenger leans towards the inside of the turn to balance the bike.

Motocross bikes

Motocross is motorcycle racing in mud! The bikes race around a bumpy, muddy course. Motocross bikes are specially made for the bumps and mud.

Built for bumps

A motocross bike has to be very strong. Its engine is higher above the ground to stop it hitting bumps. That makes motocross bikes like the Husqvarna TC450 taller than other bikes. A road bike like the Kawasaki ZX-10R is much lower. It would scrape along the bumps.

Motocross courses include hills and jumps that send the bikes flying into the air.

	Husqvarna TC450 motocross bike	Kawasaki ZX-10R sport bike
Engine:	449 cc/27 cu in	998 cc/61 cu in
Weight:	105 kg/231 lb	170 kg/375 lb
Seat height:	97 cm/3 ft 2 in	82.5 cm/2 ft 8 in
Total height:	128 cm/4 ft 2 in	111.5 cm/3 ft 8 in

128 cm/
4 ft 2 in

Springy wheels

Like all motorbikes, the engine in a motocross bike drives the back wheel. The back wheel has to stay on the ground to keep the bike going. A big spring under the seat presses the wheel down. The wheel can move up and down a long way. This allows it to follow all the humps and hollows in the ground.

The Husqvarna TC450 is a motocross bike. It has knobbly tyres. These dig into soft, muddy ground and grip better.

The most powerful racing bike

The most powerful racing bikes are **drag bikes**. Drag bikes don't race round and round a circuit. They race along a straight track, two bikes at a time.

Drag bikes are designed to go as fast as possible in a straight line. They are long and low, with very powerful engines. The fastest and most powerful are the Top Fuel bikes. They can reach a speed of more than 350 kph (220 mph) in just over six seconds!

A rider spins his bike's back wheel before a race to heat it up. A hot tyre grips the track better.

Getting a grip

Drag bikes have a big, wide back tyre. The engine drives the back wheel. The big tyre helps to grip the track better. Better grip means faster acceleration. A bike that can accelerate the fastest crosses the finish-line first.

Top Fuel drag bike

Engine:	**2,750 cc/168 cu in**
Power:	**up to 1,000 horsepower**
Top speed:	**350 kph/220 mph**
Wheelbase:	**2.3 m/7 ft 6 in**

A drag bike has a long bar called a wheelie bar at the back. This stops the bike rearing up. It also stops the bike flipping over backwards as it accelerates.

The fastest motorbikes on Earth

On Saturday 14 July, 1990, Dave Campos started the engine of his strange-looking motorcycle. He set a new **land speed record** for motorcycles of 518 kph (322 mph).

Easyriders

The motorcycle was called Easyriders. It looks like a long black tube. The rider lies down on his back inside a closed cockpit. He cannot put his feet down to steady the bike. Metal feet stick out to hold it upright. It is powered by two Harley-Davidson motorbike engines.

Motorcycles like Easyriders, shaped like long tubes, are called **streamliners**.

HEAVYWEIGHT MACHINE
Easyriders weighs more than five road bikes like the Suzuki Hayabusa.

Fastest ever

The highest speed ever reached by a motorcycle is thought to be 595 kph (370 mph). The Feuling Advanced Technologies motorcycle reached this speed in 1997.

Getting started

The world's fastest motorbikes are designed to run best at top speed. Their engines do not work very well going slowly. In fact, the bike has to be travelling at about 130 kph (80 mph) before the engine will even start! To get round this, a car or truck tows the bike up to its starting speed.

> The Feuling Advanced Technologies motorcycle is probably the world's fastest motorcycle.

	Easyriders land speed record bike	Suzuki Hayabusa road bike
Length:	7 m/23 ft	2.14 m/7 ft
Engine:	3,000 cc/182 cu in	1,299 cc/79 cu in
Weight:	1,135 kg/2,500 lb	217 kg/478 lb
Top speed:	518 kph/322 mph	312 kph/194 mph

Other extreme bikes

Before Dave Campos set the land speed record for motorcycles in 1990, the record had been held for 12 years by Don Vesco. The motorcycle used was called Lightning Bolt.

Changing name

Lightning Bolt started as a different motorcycle! It had held another land speed record and was called Silver Bird. To go even faster, it needed new engines. The new engines were bigger. Silver Bird was made longer to fit them in. The longer motorcycle with its new engines was given a new name – Lightning Bolt.

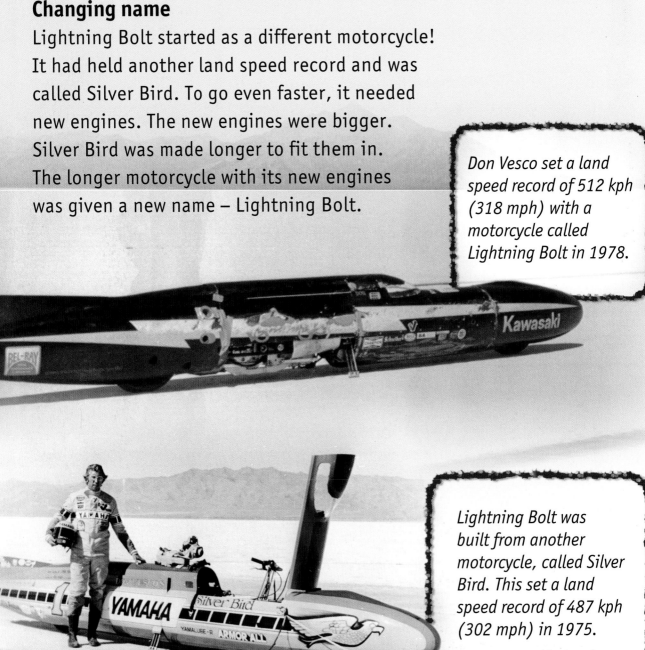

Don Vesco set a land speed record of 512 kph (318 mph) with a motorcycle called Lightning Bolt in 1978.

Lightning Bolt was built from another motorcycle, called Silver Bird. This set a land speed record of 487 kph (302 mph) in 1975.

The Dodge Tomahawk is a four-wheel monster motorcycle with a car engine!

Riding the Tomahawk

The Dodge Tomahawk is almost as fast as a land speed record motorcycle. It is a concept vehicle. This means that it has been built to show what is possible, but it may not be made in large numbers. Its huge engine usually powers a Dodge Viper supercar. To make it steadier, it has two wheels at the front and two at the back.

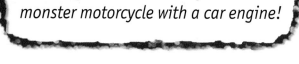

SUPERBIKE

A Dodge Tomahawk could go faster than a Formula 1 racing car! However, it would be much too difficult to ride at that speed.

	 **Dodge Tomahawk**	 **Lightning Bolt**
Type:	Concept vehicle	Land speed record bike
Engine:	8,277 cc/505 cu in	2,026 cc/124 cu in
Power:	500 horsepower	300 horsepower
Top speed:	480 kph/300 mph	513 kph/318 mph

Facts and figures

There are hundreds of types of motorcycle. Some of the world's top bikes are listed here. You can use the information to see which is the most powerful or the fastest. If you want to know more about these or other motorcycles, look on pages 30 and 31 to find out how to do some research.

Historic motorcycles	Date	Engine	Power	Top speed
Daimler Einspur (Germany)	1885	265 cc/16 cu in	0.5 horsepower	12 kph/8 mph
Indian Powerplus (USA)	1918	998 cc/61 cu in	18 horsepower	96 kph/60 mph
Harley-Davidson WL45 (USA)	1949	742 cc/45 cu in	25 horsepower	120 kph/75 mph
Triumph Bonneville (UK)	1959	649 cc/40 cu in	46 horsepower	177 kph/110 mph

Road bikes	Weight	Engine	Power	Top speed
Ducati 999R (Italy)	192 kg/423 lb	999 cc/61 cu in	150 horsepower	286 kph/178 mph
Harley-Davidson Road King (USA)	332 kg/732 lb	1,449 cc/88 cu in	66 horsepower	166 kph/103 mph
Honda CBR1000RR Fireblade (Japan)	179 kg/395 lb	998 cc/61 cu in	170 horsepower	286 kph/178 mph
Honda CBR1100XX Super Blackbird (Japan)	227 kg/500 lb	1,137 cc/69 cu in	150 horsepower	300 kph/186 mph
Kawasaki ZX-10R (Japan)	170 kg/375 lb	998 cc/61 cu in	181 horsepower	300 kph/186 mph
Suzuki GSX1300R Hayabusa (Japan)	217 kg/478 lb	1,299 cc/79 cu in	173 horsepower	312 kph/194 mph

Racing bikes	Championship	Engine	Power	Top speed *
Ducati Desmosedici (Italy)	MotoGP	989 cc/60 cu in	220 horsepower	325 kph/202 mph
Honda RC211V (Japan)	MotoGP	990 cc/60 cu in	240 horsepower	325 kph/202 mph
Yamaha YZR-M1 (Japan)	MotoGP	990 cc/60 cu in	240 horsepower	325 kph/202 mph
Ducati 999RS F05 (Italy)	Superbike	999 cc/61 cu in	194 horsepower	312 kph/194 mph
Honda CBR1000RR (Japan)	Superbike	998 cc/61 cu in	210 horsepower	312 kph/194 mph
Suzuki GSX-R1000 (Japan)	Superbike	998 cc/61 cu in	207 horsepower	312 kph/194 mph
Husqvarna TC450 (Sweden)	Motocross	449 cc/27 cu in	59 horsepower	Not known

* In the hands of top riders, some of these bikes may reach even higher speeds.

Drag bikes	Wheelbase	Engine	Power	Top speed
Top Fuel drag bike (USA)	2.3 m/7 ft 6 in	2,750 cc/168 cu in	1,000 horsepower	350 kph/220 mph
Pro Stock drag bike (USA)	1.8 m/5 ft 10 in	1,500 cc/91 cu in	300 horsepower	320 kph/200 mph

Land speed record bikes	Weight	Engine	Power	Top speed
Easyriders (USA)	1,135 kg/2,500 lb	3,000 cc/182 cu in	Not known	518 kph/322 mph
Lightning Bolt (USA)	Not known	2,026 cc/124 cu in	300 horsepower	513 kph/318 mph

Concept bikes	Weight	Engine	Power	Top speed
Dodge Tomahawk (USA)	680 kg/1,500 lb	8,277 cc/505 cu in	500 horsepower	480 kph/300 mph

The land speed record

The first motorcycle speed record of 122.14 kph (75.9 mph) was set in 1909 by William Cook on a Peugeot NLG. By 1920, motorbikes were going faster than 160 kph (100 mph). The record passed 320 kph (200 mph) in the 1950s. By then, torpedo-shaped motorcycles called streamliners were being used. They took the record above 480 kph (300 mph) in the 1970s. Today, it stands at 518.4 kph (322.1 mph).

Motorbike engines

Motorbike engines work like car engines. Fuel burns inside tube-shaped cylinders. This makes metal drums called pistons go up and down. The up and down movements are changed into a turning motion that drives the back wheel. The smallest motorbike engines have only one cylinder. A popular type of engine is the V-twin. It has two cylinders joined at the bottom to form a V shape. Other bikes have in-line engines – the cylinders are in a straight line. An in-line four engine has four cylinders in a line.

Glossary

accelerate go faster

cc cubic centimetre. A space that is one centimetre long, high, and wide. The space inside an engine where the fuel is burned is measured in cc (say 'see-sees'). The smallest motorbikes have engines of about 50 cc. The biggest road bike engine is 2,300 cc, on the Triumph Rocket III.

cruiser type of motorbike that is built more for comfort and looks than speed and performance

cu in cubic inch. A space that is one inch long, high, and wide. The space inside an engine where the fuel is burned is measured in cubic inches (cu in). The smallest motorbikes have engines of about 3 cu in. The biggest road bikes have 140 cu in engines.

cylinder part of an engine shaped like a tube. The fuel is burned here. Most motorbike engines have one, two, or four cylinders.

drag slowing effect of the air. When something tries to move through air, the air pushes back and slows it down. Some shapes cause more drag than others.

drag bike motorbike designed to go as fast as possible in a straight line

fairing a smooth cover around a motorbike. A fairing gives a bike a smoother shape so that it can slip through the air faster.

fuel substance that is burned inside a motorbike engine. Most motorbikes burn petrol. A few racing motorbikes burn special fuels that produce more power.

horsepower the power of an engine. A small motorbike might have an engine of less than 10 horsepower. A medium-sized motorbike has an engine of about 50–60 horsepower. The biggest and fastest bikes have engines of more than 150 horsepower. The most powerful drag bikes can have 1,000 horsepower engines.

land speed record the fastest speed reached by a vehicle on land. The time a motorcycle takes to go along a straight course and come back again is measured. The time is used to work out the motorcycle's speed.

MotoGP the leading world motorbike racing championship

sidecar passenger seat fixed to the side of a motorcycle. Specially built motorcycles and sidecars take part in races.

sport bike motorbike that is built for its speed and sporty (exciting) performance

streamlined the right shape to slip through the air easily. Fast motorcycles have a streamlined shape so that air flows around them smoothly and does not slow them down.

streamliner special type of motorcycle shaped like a long thin tube. Streamliners are used to set the fastest speed records.

superbike type of racing motorbike. Superbikes are similar to ordinary bikes that people can own.

tourer type of motorbike that is built for making long journeys. It has room for a passenger and luggage.

V-twin common type of motorbike engine. A V-twin has two cylinders joined at the bottom to make a V shape.

Finding out more

You can find out more about motorbikes by looking for other books to read and searching the internet.

Books
*Designed for Success – Superbike*s, by Ian Graham (Heinemann Library, 2004)

Let's Investigate – Motorcycles, by John Hudson Tiner (The Creative Company, 2003)

Wild About – Superbikes, by David Kimber (Ticktock Media, 2003)

Motorcycles online
These web sites give more information about motorcycles:

http://www.nationalmotorcyclemuseum.co.uk – the official web site of the UK National Motorcycle Museum.

http://www.motorcycle-uk.com/lmm.htm – visit this web site to find out more about London Motorcycle Museum in the United Kingdom.

http://www.nationalmcmuseum.org – this is the web site of the US National Motorcycle Museum in Anamosa, Iowa, in the United States.

http://www.motorcyclenews.com/ – the Motorcycle News web site has lots of information on all the bikes talked about in this book, plus loads of bike reviews.

More to do

New motorbikes are being designed all the time, so there are lots of different road bikes and racing bikes to find out about.

Motorcycles of the past

Famous motorcycles of the past include the Brough Superior, Harley-Davidson Model 9E, Indian Chief, FN Four, and the Norton Commando.

A famous British motorcycle of the 1950s was called the Triumph Bonneville. It was named after the Bonneville Salt Flats in the United States. Can you find out why? (Answer on page 32.)

You can also find information about record-breaking motorcycles at *http://guinnessworldrecords.com*

Index

Answer to question on page 31

The Bonneville Salt Flats in the United States are famous as a place where
speed records are set. A series of motorcycle records were set at Bonneville in
the 1950s. The motorcycles had Triumph engines. So, when Triumph created a
new motorcycle in 1959, they called it the Bonneville.

Titles in the *The World's Greatest...* series include:

Hardback 1-844-21262-9

Hardback 1-844-21263-7

Hardback 1-844-21264-5

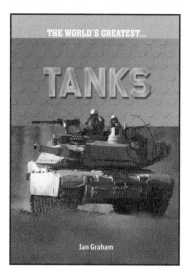

Hardback 1-844-21265-3

Hardback 1-844-21266-1

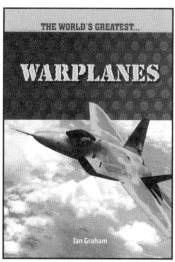

Hardback 1-844-21267-X

Find out about other titles from Raintree on our website www.raintreepublishers.co.uk